MW01051453

THE HOUSE THAT
SHE BUILT
COLORING & ACTIVITY BOOK

© 2021 Group Two Advertising, Inc.

TheHouseThatSheBuilt.com

The Architect

Connect the dots with straight lines.

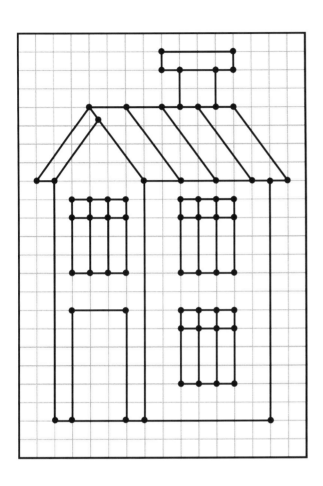 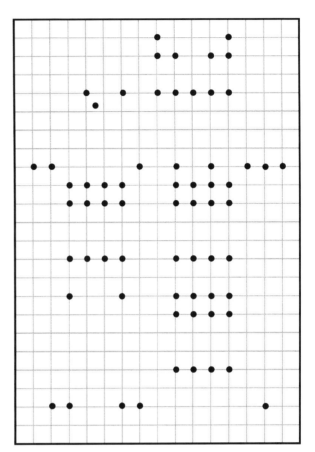

Complete the drawing based on the example.

 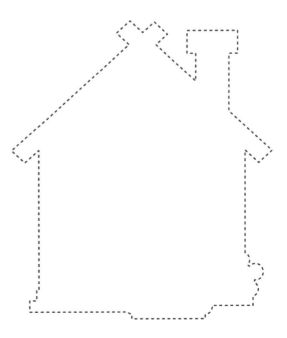

Color the shapes to represent the fraction.

$$\frac{7}{10}$$

The Engineer

The General Contractor

What time is it?

☐ o'clock

☐ o'clock

☐ o'clock

☐ o'clock

☐ o'clock

☐ o'clock

☐ o'clock

☐ o'clock

☐ o'clock

Drive the excavator to the construction site.

The House That She Built

The Excavator

The Concrete Laborer

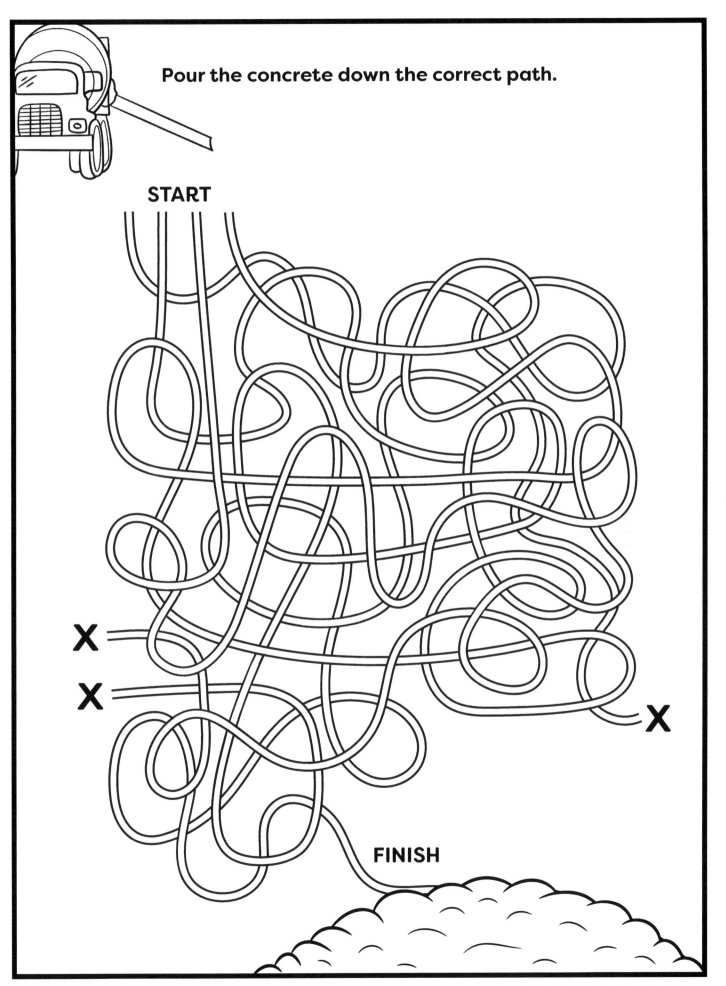

Pour the concrete down the correct path.

START

X

X

X

FINISH

Copy these patterns.

The Framer

The Electrician

Connect the plugs to the outlet.

Use the shapes to fill the grid.

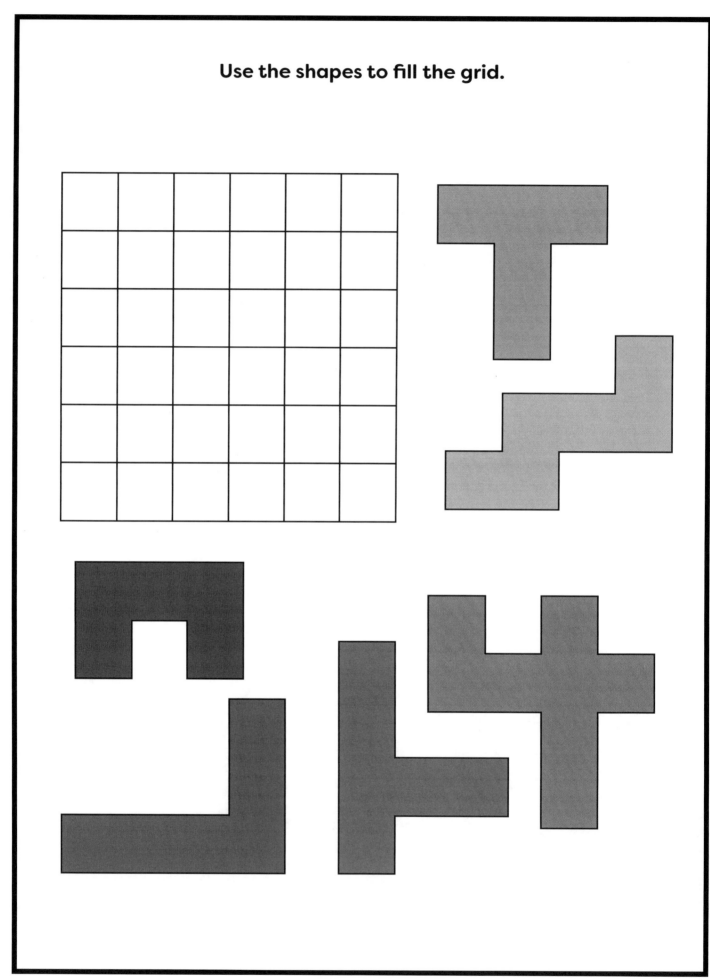

The Plumber

The HVAC Technician

Math maze! Count from 1 to 16 to circulate air through the house.

TheHouseThatSheBuilt.com

Color the butterflies.

The Roofer

The Insulation Contractor

Fill in the missing letters.

 _ _ m m e r

 _ r i l l

 s _ w

 _ u c k e _

 _ e _ e _

 _ l o _ e

What comes next?

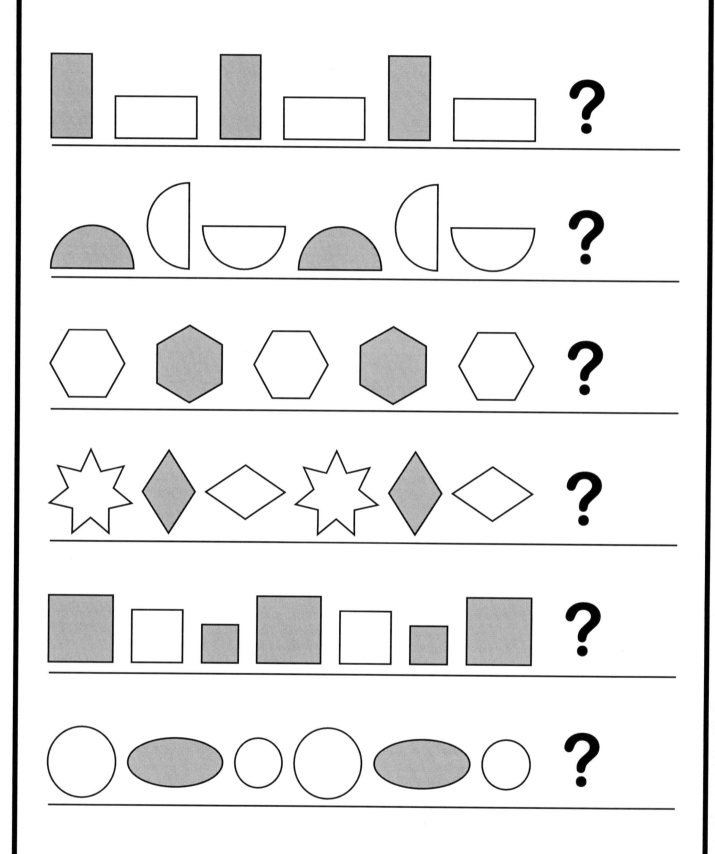

The Drywaller

The Cabinet Manufacturer

Measure the objects.

_____ in.

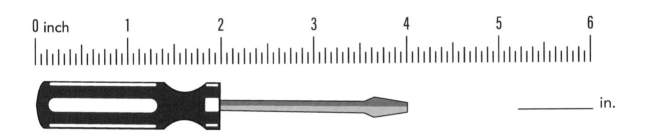

_____ in.

_____ in.

_____ in.

Redraw the windows using the grid.

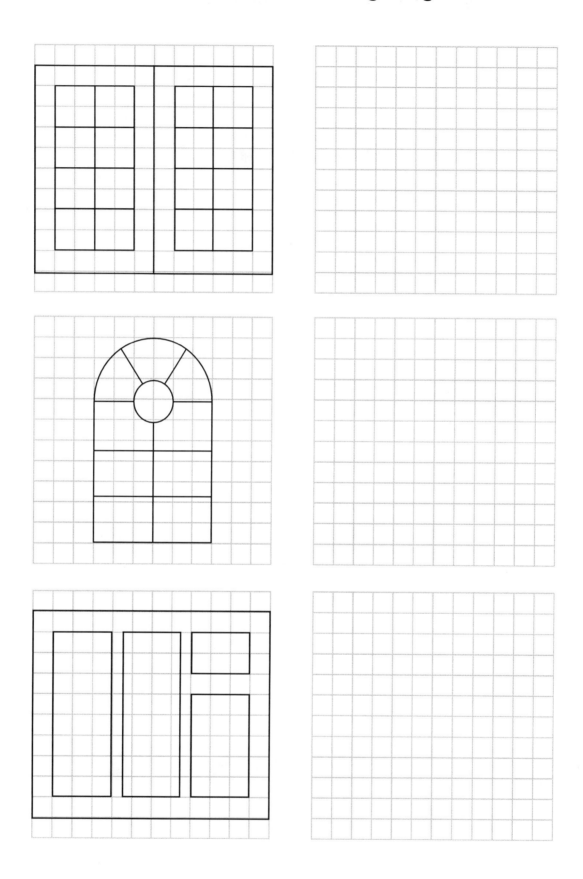

The Finish Carpenter

The Tiler

Design your own tile, then add your tile design to the sequence of tiles.

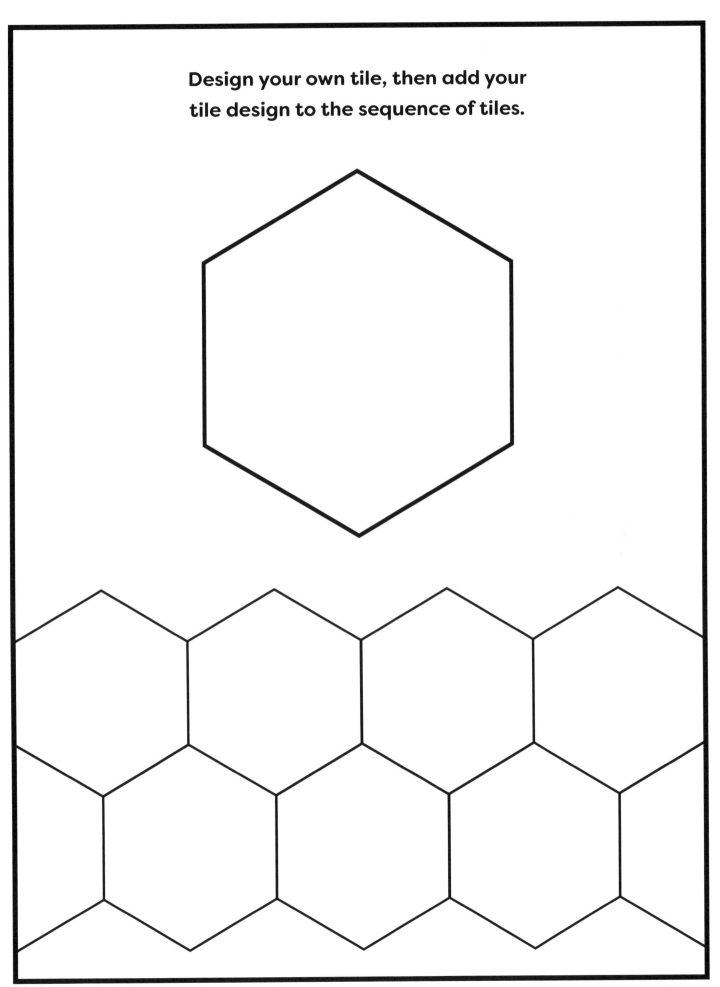

Color a "mural" on the wall of this room.

The Painter

The Interior Designer

Decorate the walls of the room. Fill it with paintings, posters, clocks, shelves, and anything else you want.

Connect each butterfly with a flower. Then color them in.

The Landscaper

The House That She Built

Design your dream house! Fill each room in this house with all of your favorite people and things.

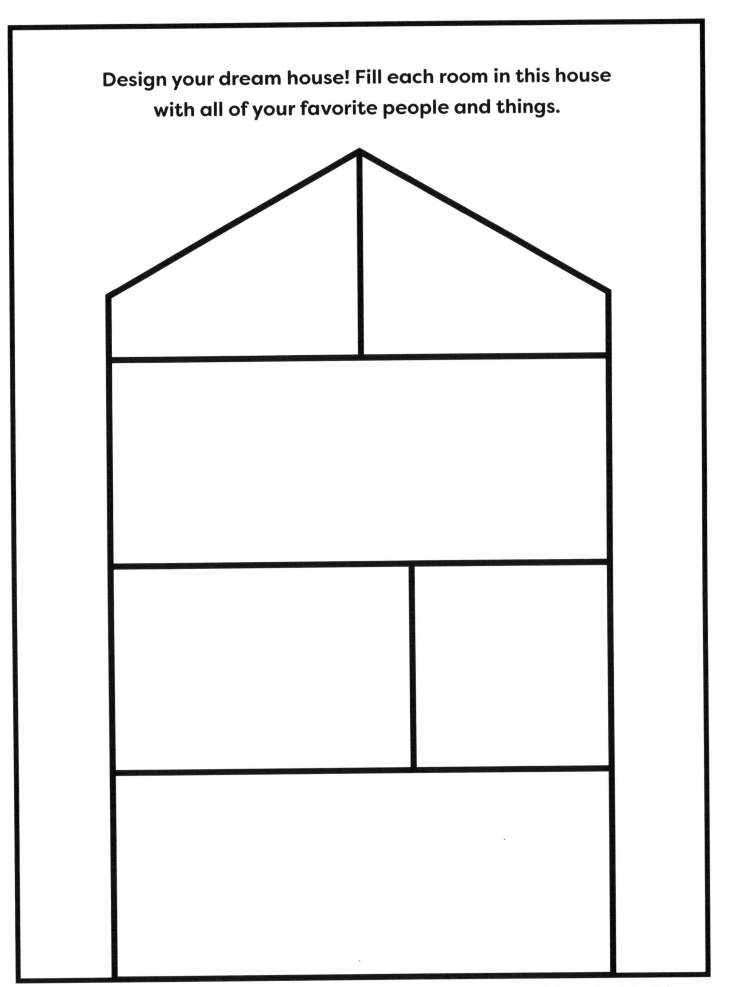

The Inspiration & Mission

The House That She Built was inspired by the team of real women who came together from around the country to build a one-of-a-kind home.

Driven by the fact that less than 3% of the onsite workforce in housing are women, the goal was to highlight and utilize skilled tradeswomen and women owned companies for all stages of the project.

Mollie Elkman and Georgia Castellano of Group Two Advertising created the brand identity and marketing for The House That She Built project, which helped secure donations, labor, and media coverage. They were so inspired by the mission that they created *The House That She Built* children's book and this Coloring & Activity book to continue sharing this important story.

The mission of *The House That She Built* is to support workforce development initiatives in home building by generating awareness of the skilled trades to all communities.

Made in the USA
Columbia, SC
01 April 2024

33878453R00024